Essential
DRUM FILLS

PETER ERSKINE

Copyright © 2008 Alfred Publishing Co., Inc.
All rights reserved. Printed in USA.

ISBN-10: 0-7390-5280-2
ISBN-13: 978-0-7390-5280-8

Contents

About the Author

Peter Erskine has been playing drums since the age of 4 and is known for his versatility and love of working in different musical contexts. He appears on over 500 albums and film scores, and has won two Grammy Awards as well as an Honorary Doctorate. He has played with (among others) the Stan Kenton and Maynard Ferguson big bands, Weather Report, Steps Ahead, Joni Mitchell, Steely Dan, Diana Krall, Kenny Wheeler, Kate Bush, The Brecker Brothers, The Yellowjackets, Pat Metheny & Gary Burton, John Scofield, Bill Frisell, Nguyên Lê, Vince Mendoza, et al, and has appeared as a soloist with the London Symphony, Los Angeles, Frankfurt Radio, Scottish Chamber, BBC Symphony and Berlin Philharmonic orchestras, as well as the radio big bands of the BBC, WDR and NDR. He is the author of several books, including *Time Awareness for All Musicians*, *Drumset Essentials*, Volumes 1, 2 & 3 and *The Erskine Method* book & DVD set, all available from Alfred Publishing. Peter is a graduate of the Interlochen Arts Academy in Michigan, and studied percussion with George Gaber at Indiana University. He was voted #1 in the Modern Drummer Magazine Readers' Poll in the Mainstream Jazz Drummer category eight times, served on the Board of Directors for the Percussive Arts Society for many years, and is a Resource Team member and contributor to the International Association of Jazz Educators. He is the designer of several innovative percussion products, including his signature "Ride Stick" model (available form Vic Firth, Inc.), and the "Stand-Alone" Stickbag (manufactured by Drum Workshop). Professor Erskine is the Director of Drumset Studies at the University of Southern California. His website is www.petererskine.com.

Notation Legend

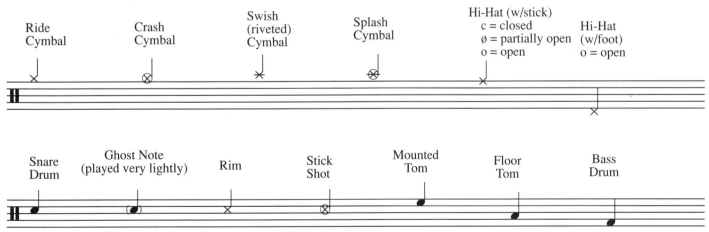

Essential Drum Fills

What is a fill?

A drum fill is a short solo that:

1. is played in time

2. carries the music forward

   a. this could be while keeping time during a song

   b. playing "behind" (accompanying) a soloist

   c. playing between the band's written figures in an arrangement

3. is played in the style of the music

4. provides a musical groove

5. can provide excitement...plus the unexpected!

Drum fills can be simple, or they can be complicated. Fills must be played in time with the rest of the music. The best drum fills provide enough rhythmic information to the rest of the band so that the other musicians can continue playing their best (without getting nervous or wondering where the beat is). Fills are timekeeping deluxe. In short, drum fills are musical moments where the drummer can express their own personality.

Essential Drum Fills is a collection of fills that I have enjoyed hearing and/or playing over the years. Each fill will be presented with its target, or destination point. A drum fill will always have a target. Getting there can be simple. The drummer may also play the sort of fill that is complex, or completely unexpected. Which fills sound good or work the best? This is up to you, the drummer. The best way to know is to listen to enough music and drummers so you can decide what you'd like to play.

Fills will be presented in two basic styles: jazz (swung 8th-notes, i.e., triplet-based rhythms), and popular music—pop, rock, fusion, funk, etc.—(straight 8th-notes).

It is recommended that the student go through the exercises in the order they are presented. Practice at different tempos, beginning at a comfortable and steady pace.

Let's get started.

Four suggested ways to approach the learning of drum fills are:

1. Listen

2. Serve (play for) the music.

3. Practice all of the fills in this book.

4. Have fun.

Many of the fill exercises in this book can be edited by the player, leaving out notes here and there in order to create more space within the fill. Once you master the mechanics, use your imagination and your ears!

Fills

Drum fills do not exist in a vacuum. An effective or good-sounding fill takes the music from where it has been to where it's going.

We can practice fills on their own in order to work out and perfect the required stickings, hand, arm and foot movements. But it's best to play fills in a musical context. It is within this context that you'll best figure out **what** to play **where**.

Whatever style of music you're playing, you can construct fills in one of the following three ways:

1. Play something you've heard another drummer play (and this is okay!).

2. Play something new.

3. Choose **NOT** to play a fill, and focus purely on the TIME for the moment.

LISTENING can teach us the most when it comes to (re)creating and playing fills. Some musical styles seem to naturally invite particular fills at a particular moment—so, whether your inspiration comes from Philly Joe Jones or Jeff Porcaro, the chances are great that their drumming ideas will serve you well.

Here is a Top 10 list of famous drum fills—highly recommended listening:

1. Shadow Wilson's fill on the Count Basie recording *Queer Street*. Buddy Rich said of this fill: "This is the most perfect drum break ever recorded." — *Wild*

2. Buddy Rich's heart-stopping break on *Love for Sale* ("Big Swing Face," 1966); super-human single strokes for three bars, and then one second of silence. — *Bliss!*

3. Tony Williams' fills on *Seven Steps to Heaven* (from Miles Davis' 'live' album, "Four & More"); be-bop vocabulary turned upside down and inside-out. — *Fun*

4. The signature "Motown" drum fill; perfect for the song, every time. — *Groovy*

5. Mel Lewis' use of dead-sticking (resting the sticks on or pressing the sticks into the snare or tom head while playing) on most of his fills. — *Hip*

6. Sonny Payne's fills on *Cute* with Count Basie's Big Band. — *Cute!*

7. Steve Gadd's fills on the Steely Dan tune *Aja*. — *Awesome*

8. Philly Joe Jones' fills on *Danny Boy*. — *Witty and swinging*

9. Bernard Purdie's break on Aretha Franklin's *Rock Steady*. — *Funky*

10. Any fills by Don Lamond, Baby Dodds, Max Roach, Art Blakey, and Airto. — *Great*

Some time-keeping fills are like conversational chance takers. The drummer might not be sure how much space they have in which to speak, but their interjection should certainly be part of the conversation. When it comes to pre-arranged charts, the drummer's options are more clear cut: We can either play up until the next tutti[1] entrance (for example, the downbeat or **TARGET**), or the drummer can play through the figure (or over the bar line).

---

[1] When the ensemble plays a passage as a whole.

Four Questions

1. Should we also be aware of the relative dynamics of the music when we play a fill? Should the fill be played loud or soft?

2. Is there a difference between the type of fill that occurs during or between an ensemble's musical phrases, and a fill that occurs all on its own without any other instruments playing? In other words, what's the difference between a *fill* and a *solo*?

3. What kind of inner dynamics can we utilize in a fill? In other words, how many accents should we add to a rhythm, and where?

4. When playing TIME, how often should we "fill?"

Four Answers

1. If we're truly listening to the music we're playing, then we're aware of the relative dynamics, and we would honor and observe these dynamics. I call it "meeting the energy of the style of music" that we're playing. The use of loud or soft can have a musically dramatic effect, and contrast can be a good idea. Short answer: Use your ears.

2. Short answer: Everything is timekeeping, and it's all music! Longer answer: A fill is much like the next step you take when walking, while a solo is more like doing a tap dance. Whether you choose to add the juggling of flaming bowling pins to the routine is up to you.

3. Notes without accents are like syllables or words without inflection (or, like food without spice). In other words, boring. Accents bring music to life and give shape to musical phrases. Just like all of the other drumming decisions you'll be making when you play, listening and experience will be your best guides. Personally, getting the "flavor" just right has become the most interesting thing about drumming. Your fills will just keep getting better, trust me.

4. A few years ago, I asked Brazilian pianist Eliane Elias to provide a quote for my first instructional book. Her contribution was "Don't play a fill every two bars." Good advice!

Four Thoughts

1. Inspiration comes from the music (i.e., use motivic elements of the chart or from the other players' improvisations).

2. Inspiration will also come from your instrument, so create a dialogue between the various parts of your kit (e.g., ask a question on your snare drum, and then answer it with a cymbal crash and bass drum!). Experiment with orchestration on the kit. Destination points, or accents, can be played on the snare drum, bass drum, crash cymbal, or a combination (usually in pairs).

3. Honor the spaces between the notes you play (i.e., don't "cheat" the beat).

4. Use the element of surprise when appropriate.

Swing Feel

The written eighth note is swung in jazz…

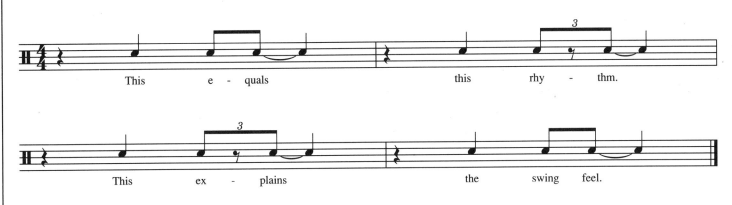

Destination Points & Variation

Fills can be played up to the destination point, or can land on or establish a strong beat as a set-up before the target point or entrance of the band.

Your fills can also play through or past the destination point, "answering" the ensemble accent with one of your own.

One of the more common rhythms the drummer will be asked to "set up," by means of a fill, is for the entrance of the band on the + of beat 4. Here are a dozen typical variations you can try on the play-along track *Rhythm Method*.

Some of these will work better than others, depending on the tempo or the energy of the piece.

Please remember: As far as other musicians are concerned, timekeeping is the most important part of drumming. Always play in such a way that will make the other musicians sound better. Your fills should help create a comfortable **AND** exciting musical zone, as there will be times when you'll need to bring in players who have been waiting to play (during a long solo section, for example). Because their instruments might be cold or their attention level not at 100%, this would not be a good time to play a lead-in figure that's confusing.

Fills can be played in-between ensemble figures as stand-alone statements. This type of filling is commonly referred to as "playing the holes."

Band figures written...

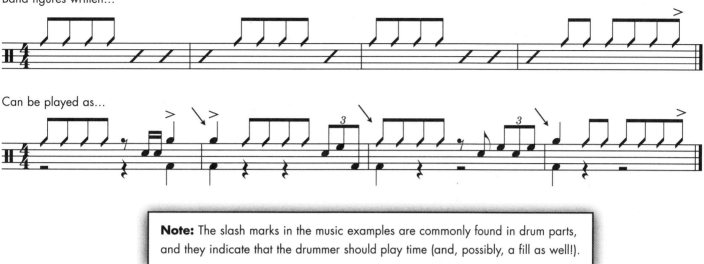

Can be played as...

Embellishments can add some nice color and shape to a fill. Contrast these three examples of pop fills:

The essence of the fill remains the same, but the added flourish of the sixteenth-note sextuplet figure makes the rhythm, well, "sextupletier."

You'll have the opportunity to try out many different fills in the following pages, so practice them all at different dynamics and tempos. In some cases, stickings are provided. It's best, however, for the student to figure out their own stickings on the kit (e.g., which part of the kit, and when to play a double-stroke in order to easily move from one part of the kit to another). As you create more and more of your own fills, you'll need to create your own stickings on the fly.

It is recommended that you play **TIME** between each exercise.

Triplets, Swing Feel

#1 (w/drums)
#2 (w/o drums)

Destination Point = 4+

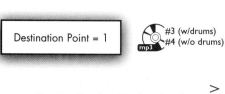

Destination Point = 1

#3 (w/drums)
#4 (w/o drums)

Destination Point = 1+

#5 (w/drums)
#6 (w/o drums)

Destination Point = 2

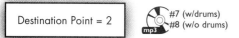
#7 (w/drums)
#8 (w/o drums)

Destination Point = 4

#11 (w/drums)
#12 (w/o drums)

Destination Point = 4 (with quarter-note set-up)

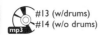
#13 (w/drums)
#14 (w/o drums)

Sixteenths, Swing Feel

#15 (w/drums)
#16 (w/o drums)

Destination Point = 4 (with quarter-note set-up)

Destination Point = 4

#17 (w/drums)
#18 (w/o drums)

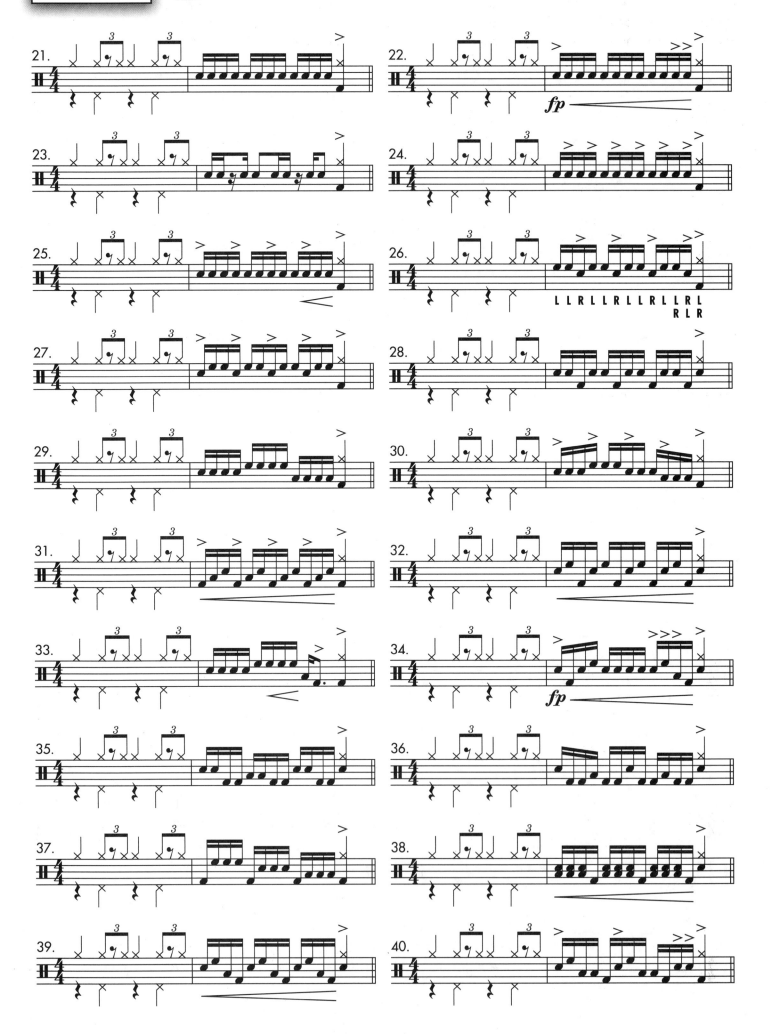

Destination Point = 1

#19 (w/drums)
#20 (w/o drums)

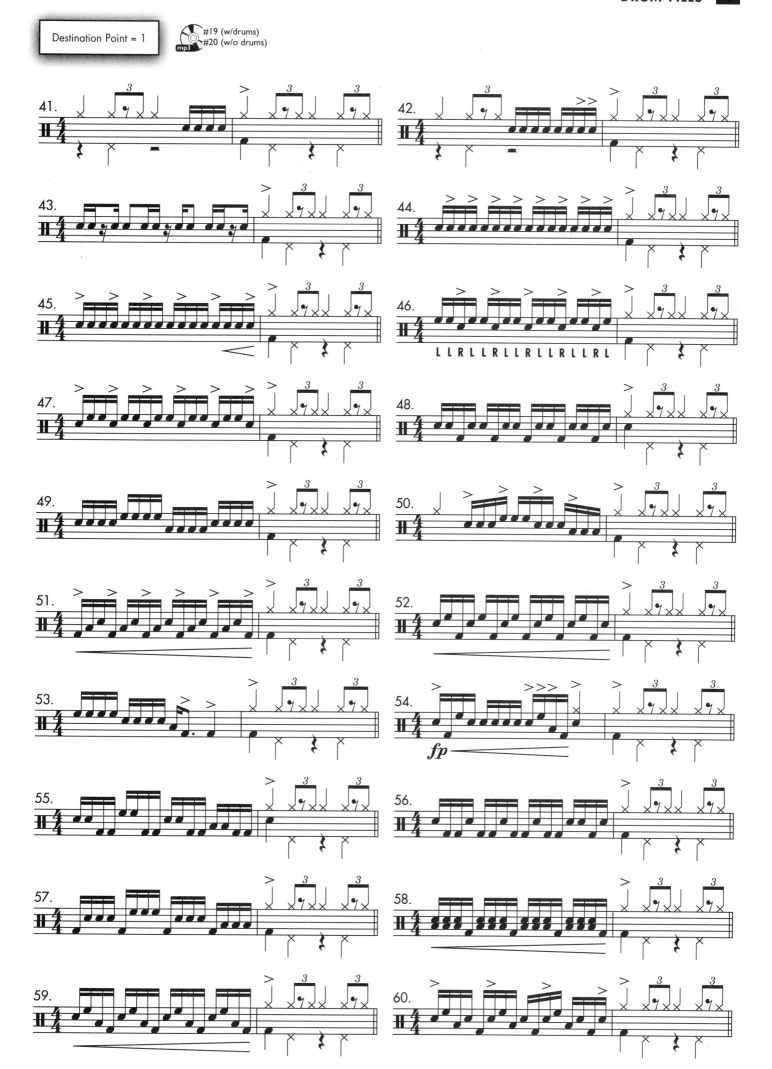

Destination Point = 1+

#21 (w/drums)
#22 (w/o drums)

Destination Point = 4+

#23 (w/drums)
#24 (w/o drums)

Destination Point = 2

#25 (w/drums)
#26 (w/o drums)

Eighth Notes, Triplets, Sixteenths & Beyond

Sixteenths & Straight Eighth-Note Feel

Destination Point = 4 (with quarter-note set-up)

#27 (w/drums)
#28 (w/o drums)

Destination Point = 4

#29 (w/drums)
#30 (w/o drums)

Destination Point = 1

#31 (w/drums)
#32 (w/o drums)
mp3

Destination Point = 1+

#33 (w/drums)
#34 (w/o drums)

Destination Point = 4+

#35 (w/drums)
#36 (w/o drums)

Eighths & Straight Eighth-Note Feel

#39 (w/drums)
#40 (w/o drums)

Destination Point = 4

Destination Point = 1

#41 (w/drums)
#42 (w/o drums)

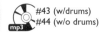

Destination Point = 4+   #43 (w/drums)
#44 (w/o drums)

Fusion-style fills on top of a medium-slow **VAMP** (*repeating phrase*).
#47 (w/drums)
#48 (w/o drums)

Practice the following rhythms on the snare drum while playing the simple ostinato on the bass drum and hi-hat. Once you get comfortable with the various subdivisions and accents, begin to combine them while moving the voices around the drumset. You'll be creating your own short solo and fill ideas in no time. In time, I mean…

Ostinatos for practicing the following improvisational ideas

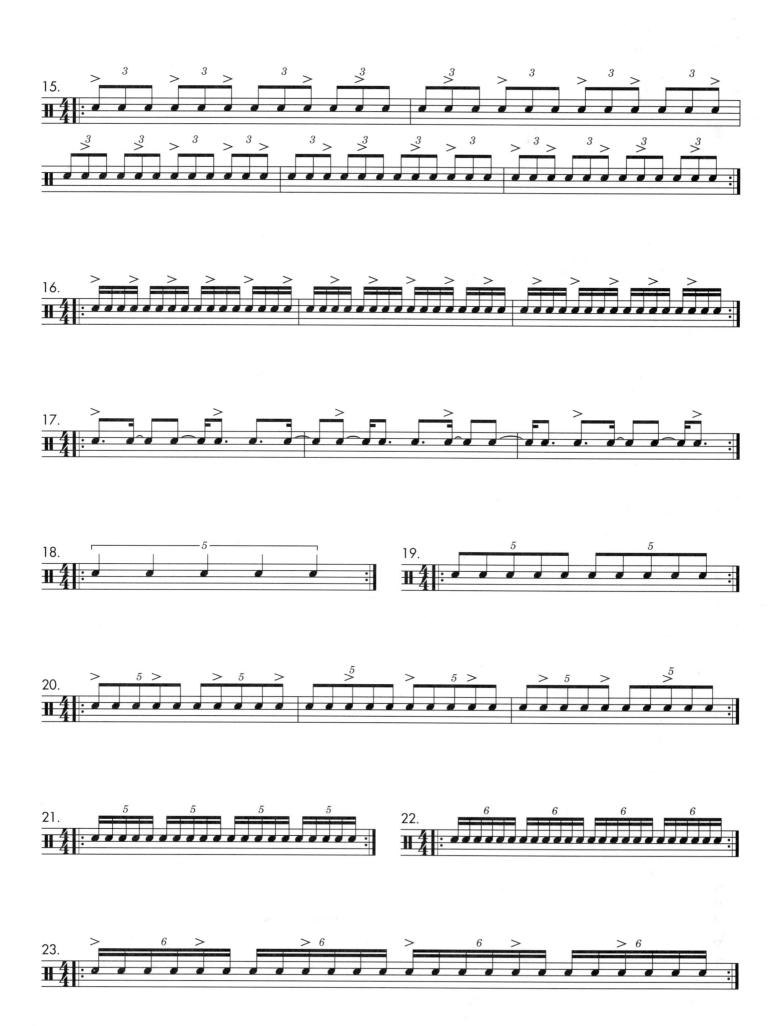

In addition to practicing different rhythmic groupings over an ostinato, the drummer can use time-honored musical development techniques such as the following:

Call and Response:

Theme and Variations:

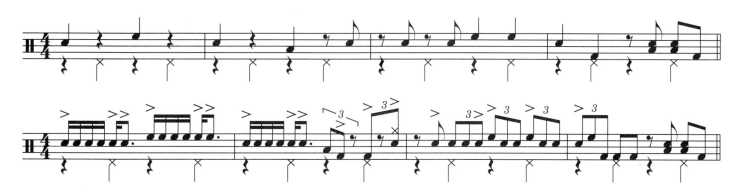

Adding dynamic variations and contrast:

Here's a mathematical equation for you:

$$FILLS + FILLS + FILLS = A\ SOLO$$

Check out the transcription, beginning on the following page, of the Max Roach solo on *Sing, Sing, Sing* (from the classic drum battle album "Rich vs. Roach"). Max played a drum solo that's made up of rhythmic motifs using the high-to-low drums (i.e., playing melodically and compositionally). These melodic riffs would make excellent fills on most any jazz setting. In fact, Max's drum solo is melodic enough for the most part to be a saxophone solo.

Sing, Sing, Sing
(Rich vs. Roach)

Max Roach Solo
(1:52–3:39)

Transcribed by
Matt Slocum

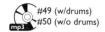
#49 (w/drums)
#50 (w/o drums)

Boogie Shuttle Stop
(Trading 8ths)

Transcribed by
Matt Slocum

*1 – Not phrased exactly as written (a little bit uneven/staggered)

*2 – x = on the rim

*3 – ⊘ = Stick Shot (stick on stick)
x = on rim

The following two pages contain the complete drumset parts for two big band charts I recorded with trumpeter Wayne Bergeron's big band. When I was in the studio, sight-reading these charts during the one run-through before we recorded the tunes (both of them in one "take"), I tried to adhere to one of the golden rules of reading a piece of music: It's just as important to have a good pair of ears as a good pair of eyes when sight-reading! Reading lets you know what the rest of the band is doing, but it's up to your ears and experience to determine what will work best for the music. The beauty of drumming is that we get to make choices, almost all of the **TIME**.

Intro to "Rhythm Method" & possible other choices:

Additional introduction choices:

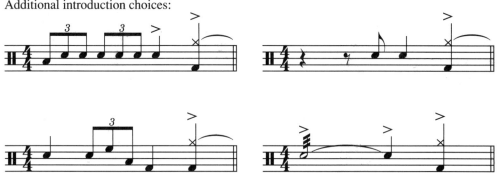

"Waltz of the Flower" fill at measures 3 and 4 of letter S, and possible alternatives:

Listen to the reference tracks and read along (pages 43 & 44) either before *or* after you play the chart with the band on the CD yourself!

#51 (w/drums)
#52 (w/o drums)

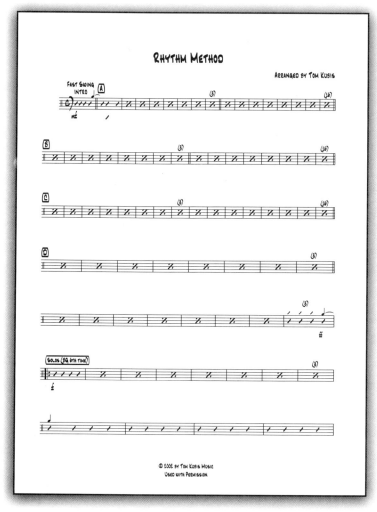

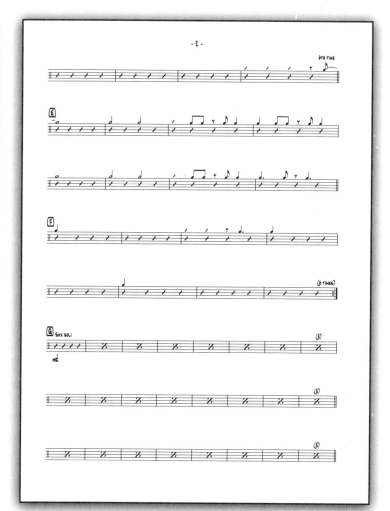

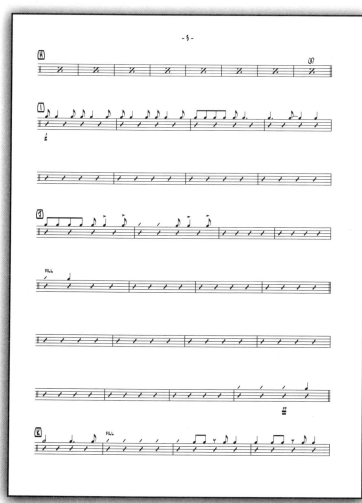

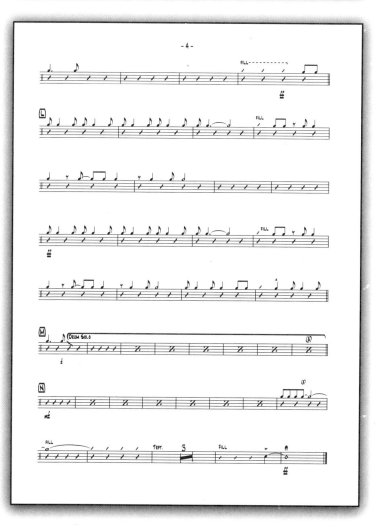

#53 (w/drums)
#54 (w/o drums)

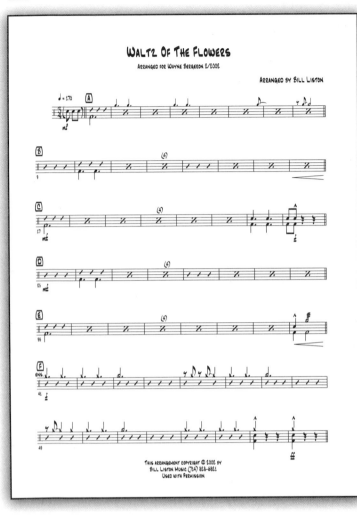

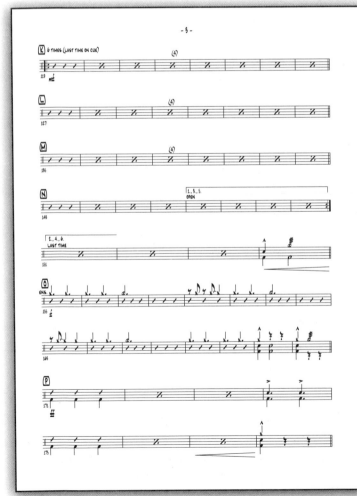

Advanced Fill Concepts

1. Individual notes can be embellished:

Flams:

Drags:

Ruffs:    Can be played as a triplet, or as 32nd notes:

Single-hand multiple strokes, or buzz roll.

> **Note:** Be careful not to overuse this device. The single-hand buzz roll has a tendency to sound like a decrescendo.

2. "Dead-Sticking" + "Ghost Notes" (normally notated in parentheses)

This is a technique where the stick or brush is played on the head without rebounding off the head (i.e., played "into" the head). This changes the tone of the drum and the texture of the fill. Mel Lewis utilized this technique often. "Ghost notes" are just that, phantom notes that are almost played and heard, but not really (soft notes, in fact).

3. Play on the Outline

This is the type of fill where there are multiple destination points (i.e., accents). These frameworks give shape to a drummer's fills while allowing him or her to utilize "long tones" in the form of rolls or indeterminate stickings (á la Jack DeJohnette). Such fills do not depend so much on set or predetermined stickings as they do on the drummer creating musical phrases and "filling" the spaces between the multiple accent points.

Outline

Long Tones on Outline

> Experiment with these types of devices.
> Your fills will become three-dimensional.

Here are some more fills where the outline rhythm is written first, followed by one possible interpretation in the style of Elvin Jones. The suggested stickings are just that—suggestions. The main idea is to get a rolling effect from drum-to-drum while providing "time" by means of the accented notes (outline). Use your imagination, and your ears, and let your hands follow. Meanwhile, practice these with and without a metronome!

The following pages contain two charts: The first is a trio tune (lead sheet) written by Alan Pasqua that has a drum solo (transcribed), and the second is a big band arrangement (by Tim Hagans) of a composition of mine titled *Worth the Wait*. Follow both charts while listening to the performances on the enclosed CD (there is also a play-along version of the trio tune for you to practice with). Performance notes appear after the big band chart.

#55 (w/drums)
#56 (w/o drums)
mp3

Daddy, What Is God's Last Name?

Alan Pasqua

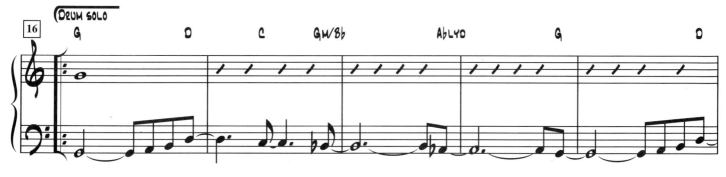

(D.C. al Fine)

Pino solo 1, 11
Drum solo 16

#55 (w/drums)

Daddy, What Is God's Last Name?

(Peter Erskine's Drum Solo at Measure 16)

Transcribed by
Matt Slocum

(2:56 4:05)

*1 = Lightly Swung   *2 = Phrased with a staggered triplet feel.

From the Fuzzy Music CD *Worth the Wait*, Peter Erskine & Tim Hagans, and the Norrbotten Big Band.

#57 (w/drums)

Performance notes: Peter Erskine's drumming on *Worth the Wait*

The tune starts out with an open alto saxophone solo and rhythm section; the band will come in on cue. The form of the tune equals 32 bars. I am playing brushes at the beginning of the tune; the bass is playing in "2" for a couple of choruses while the drums chug away in "4." This creates a nice feel. I play a triplet fill which musically indicates to the bass player that it would be a good idea to go into a more intense "walking 4." The piano also comes in after this set-up. During the entire time of the solo, as well as the band's tutti, the drums play in an interactive way, and all fills are played with timekeeping in mind. I utilize something that Chick Webb did a long time ago with his band on the tune *Don't Be That Way* when I anticipate or echo the ensemble's accented hits with off-beat counterpoints on the drums [mm. 122–126]. The fill seems to be part of the arrangement. This is a good example (and another way) of filling in the holes.

We decided to insert a drum solo into the arrangement. I play a single chorus and cue the band back in, both by the phrase I play as well as by making eye contact with the other players in the rhythm section. Switching to sticks during the piano solo, the feel "builds" in intensity, through the flugelhorn solo on up to the band's entrance for the second shout chorus. As the writing is fairly "busy" here, I decided to keep the fills to a minimum and orient the drumming more around "time" than anything else.

Four Famous Fills:

Back to some of those famous drum fills I mentioned at the beginning of the book…

1. Shadow Wilson's fill on the Count Basie recording *Queer Street*. Buddy Rich said of this fill: "This is the most perfect drum break ever recorded." What's noteworthy is the brilliantly unexpected use of the double-time syncopation in the second bar of the fill.

2. Buddy Rich's heart-stopping break on *Love for Sale* ("Big Swing Face," 1966); super-human single strokes for three bars, and then one second of silence before the band comes back in. — *Bliss!*

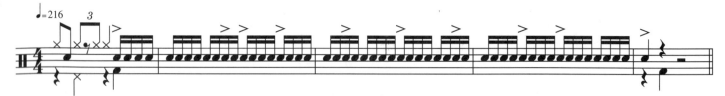

3. Tony Williams' fills on *Seven Steps to Heaven* (from Miles Davis' 'live' album *Four & More*); be-bop vocabulary turned upside down and inside-out. — *Hip!*

4. The signature "Motown" drum fill; perfect for just about every Motown song, every time.

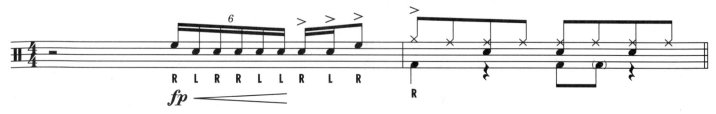

Afterword

I hope you will enjoy and benefit from this book. Here's some additional advice:

Music is the best teacher, so listening is the best way to learn.

Some fills will be short solos, and some will be timekeeping with that something extra added! Accents, syncopations, "bombs" (loud and sometimes unexpected, like the kind such bebop pioneers as Kenny Clarke, Max Roach and Art Blakey often played), etc., are all part of the vocabulary. Try to use motivic elements of the song or arrangement when possible, and, if in doubt, stay in character with the tune.

Fast tempos will usually mean less notes, not more — speed alone does not make for more intensity.

Musical intensity will come from being able to play subdivisions with great specificity and control, and then using that specificity and control to warp or more fully express the moment, by means of changing the volume as well as speed intensity (like a racing car going around a curve: zzzZZOOOOOmm!).

Finally, this thought:

"Sometimes the best fill is no fill at all."

Santa Monica, California 2008

Credits

Wayne Bergeron Big Band: *Rhythm Method* and *Waltz of the Flowers* from "You Call This a Living?"
CD label: Wag Wecords
Catalog No.: WB-1002
Leader/trumpet soloist: Wayne Bergeron
Trumpets and flugelhorns: Warren Luening, Rick Baptist, Dennis Farias, Larry Hall, Deborah Wagner
Trombones: Charlie Loper, Andy Martin, Bruce Otto, Bill Reichenbach
Saxophones: Dan Higgins, Greg Huckins (alto & flute); Bill Liston & Jeff Driskill (tenor & flute);
Jay Mason (baritone & flute)
Piano: Alan Pasqua
Bass: Chuck Berghofer
Drums: Peter Erskine
Executive Producer: Gary Grant
Associate Producers: Andy Waterman, Wayne Bergeron
Recorded at The Bakery Digital Sound & Vision
Engineered by: Andy Waterman; Mixed by: Andy Waterman, Gary Grant, Wayne Bergeron
Mastered by: Damon A. Tedesco of Mobile DISC & D.A.T.

Piano trio tracks: *Daddy, What Is God's Last Name?* and *Boogie Shuttle Stop* from "Badlands"
CD label: Fuzzy Music (fuzzymusic.com)
Catalog No.: PEPCD011
Piano: Alan Pasqua
Bass: Dave Carpenter
Drums: Peter Erskine
Full-band versions recorded by Brian Risner at Puck Productions, Santa Monica, CA
Mixed and mastered by Rich Breen
Produced by Peter Erskine
Above titles without drums recorded and mixed by Brian Risner at Puck Productions

Worth the Wait (Peter Erskine, arranged by Tim Hagans) from "Worth the Wait"
CD label: Fuzzy Music (fuzzymusic.com)
Catalog No.: PEPCD015
Soloists: Johan Hörlén (as), Peter Erskine (dr), Daniel Tilling (pno), Dan Johansson (tpt)
Conductor & Trumpet: Tim Hagans
Saxophones: Håkan Broström, Johan Hörlén, Mats Garberg, Bengt Ek, Per Moberg
Trombones: P-O Svanström, Magnus Puls, Peter Dahlgren, Björn Hängsel (b.tb)
Trumpets: Bo Strandberg, Dan Johansson, Magnus Ekholm, Tapio Maunuvaara
Piano: Daniel Tilling
Guitar: Ola Bengtsson
Bass: Martin Sjöstedt
Drums: Peter Erskine
Recording produced by Lars-Göran Ulander for Sveriges Radio P2 (Swedish Radio), Tim Hagans & Peter Erskine for Fuzzy Music;
NBB Producer: Mirka Siwek
Engineer: Bo Andersin; Remix & Mastering Engineer: Rich Breen

Drum tracks and play-along loops recorded by Rich Breen at Puck Productions
Drums: Peter Erskine
Bass: Dave Carpenter
Piano: Hajime Yoshizawa

Thanks to: The 2007–2008 class of jazz drumming students at USC, Alan Pasqua, Dave Carpenter, Dave Black, Matt Slocum, Steve Fidyk, Wayne Bergeron, Tom Kubis, Bill Liston, and everyone at Alfred Publishing.